A GUIDE TO STARTING AND RUNNING A SMALL BUSINESS.

By David Ashdown FIoEE

If you have a great idea, hobby or interest that you would like to turn into a business, then this guide is for you.

DAA Consulting
11 Greenleaf House
Darkes Lane
Potters Bar
Hertfordshire, EN6 1AE

01707 527725
office@daa.consulting
www.daa.consulting

A GUIDE TO STARTING AND RUNNING A SMALL BUSINESS

By David Ashdown FIoEE

*"The best way to predict your
future is to create it"
— Peter F. Drucker*

About the Author

In 1974, whilst still at school and at the grand old age of 13, David started his first business. Three months earlier he had started a Saturday job cleaning windows for a local firm and had quickly realized that the company offered little in terms of customer satisfaction.

"The owner simply wanted me to rush from house to house as quickly as possible, so that he could collect as much money as possible", David recalls. *"Customers often complained and I got the brunt of it as the owner was never around. He would drop me off at the start of the day and then collect me at the end and all he was interested in, was how much money I had collected. When I told him so-and-so were unhappy, he would just shrug it off and say there were plenty more customers around".*

Disillusioned, David realized there had to be a better way and spoke to one of the full time guys. *"Dan was older than me, had a car, some ladders and the same disillusioned frustration as me but didn't have the confidence to approach customers and start out on his own".*

It was a perfect match, David had no shyness in *'knocking on doors'* so in July 1974 Dave and Dan started their own round. Dan supplied the vehicle and materials and David found the work, and with their combined belief of *'keeping the customer satisfied'*, they gained just as many new customers through recommendation as they did by cold calling.

By 1976, Dave and Dan had built up a solid round *"even though school often got in the way!"* David says jokingly, and had accumulated a *'tidy sum of money'* simply by offering great customer service. Plans had been hatched to expand into office & industrial cleaning, until his father put a stop to it all and told him to 'get a proper job'.

Reluctantly, David sold his share to Dan and took a job in Estate Agency in North London but within a few years he had the urge again *to 'go it alone'* and in 1981 he started buying, converting and renovating old houses and selling them on for a profit.

David achieved solid success throughout the 1980's dealing in an impressive portfolio of property transactions, including the development of an early Tesco Superstore and the relocation of an NHS Hospital. During this time, David established himself as a successful entrepreneur and property developer. In 1988, recognizing the vulnerability of the property market, David cashed-in and sold off his property interests before the market plunged into a deep recession.

Through a friend and business colleague, David was offered an opportunity to take over an ailing transport company, which he believed had substantial scope for growth. With little or no knowledge of the industry, David threw himself into it and subsequently grew it by over 1000% in 12 years, expanding into logistics, storage, vehicle hire and distribution. In 2001, David exited the business and set up his own consultancy practice.

Since then, David has acted as a business consultant, advisor and mentor to a number of SME's and is also an approved Chartered Management Institute Tutor, delivering Degrees and Diplomas in Leadership & Management to senior management and business owners and sits on the Board of a number of small businesses as a Non-Executive Director.

He is also an accredited member of the ibd-group, a Fellow of the Institute of Enterprise & Entrepreneurs and a member of The Association of Business Mentors as well as Enterprise Nation.

David is a strong-minded yet affable character with excellent people skills with key strengths in marketing, negotiation, mediation and business development.

Born in 1961 in North London, David has been married for 27 years, is a father to three daughters and a grandfather to one and now lives in Hertfordshire. He is a keen Motor Racing fan and Rugby supporter.

"Everyone has an idea but it's really about executing that idea and attracting other people to help you work on it that counts".

TABLE of Contents

Introduction

Hello and welcome to my guide on how to start and run a small business. This guide is intended for use as a short reference and is not in any way exhaustive. There are many factors affecting how you start and run your own business but I hope you will find this book a handy guide to some of the basic principles.

For some, starting a business can be daunting and for others, it's a case of; they can't wait to get started. Either way, it is always good to remember that there is lots of help and advice out there and not only can that advice prove invaluable, it doesn't have to cost the earth. Treat all forms of advice as an invaluable investment into your business.

I believe, that anyone looking at running their own business is an Entrepreneur because Entrepreneurs take resources and make things happen. That is exactly what you are doing by running your own business.

Remember though, it's not just about having an idea. It's about implementing it. I have seen people with great ideas fail, and conversely I have seen others with what appears a poor idea, become a success.

Drive and ambition are key ingredients in Entrepreneurship but that said, it's always good to listen to others. If there really isn't a demand for your idea, there is no point in flogging a dead horse just because you want to prove others wrong.

Entrepreneurs are more innovative, leading to new products and services being created, which in turn leads to lower unemployment and an enhancement of lifestyles. So what makes a good entrepreneur?

It is generally recognised that the Attributes or Traits of an Entrepreneur are fundamentally:

- Ambition (the need to succeed),
- Creativity (always innovative),
- Tenacity (often stubborn),
- Risk Tolerant (being bold),
- Intuition (spontaneous) and
- Personality (the life and soul).

To understand the background to entrepreneurship, lets look a little at where it all started:

The first recorded entrepreneurs were in medieval days (the church, merchants and members of the royal court), who introduced new goods with new quality and value.

Then, people came off the land and into industry with the development of the Cotton Mills and the Industrial Revolution. From this came the Flying Shuttle, Spinning Jenny, Water Frame and Crompton's 'Mule'.

Entrepreneurship led to enterprise, innovation and organisational skills.

Today there are 4.9 million businesses in the UK, employing 24.3 million people with a combined turnover of £3.6 trillion and entrepreneurship is seen as a major future driver of economic growth in the economy.

So whatever stage you are at, by being an Entrepreneur and starting your own business, you are helping to build a future for you, your future generation and the UK.

Well done and welcome to the world of business and entrepreneurship. I hope you find this guide helpful.

With special thanks to all those who have contributed to this guide, especially Geraldine Scott for her various blogs and research.

Thank you for reading.

David Ashdown

David Ashdown FIoEE

One - STARTING A BUSINESS

Starting a business can be both exciting and scary. It's a big undertaking and a big step. You have the idea, you have the skill but do you have the time and do you have the finance, and most importantly, have you done your research?

It s a sad fact that most small businesses fail within the first year. Many fail though, because they have not set out their stall correctly nor planned ahead.

This guide will hopefully help you in not making some of the classic mistakes when starting out:

Market Validation – IS there a Market?

It goes almost without saying, but the most fundamental starting point for creating a business is an idea. However, not all good ideas become good businesses. But to begin with, you must ask yourself, **is there a market for this idea?**

If not, why not? Is it because you have discovered or identified a niche, or is it because there is no demand? It is very important to try and identify which one it is. I have met many people who believe that their idea is 'the next best thing'.

They tell me this because they have come up with an idea, which is unique that no one else is doing.

Because no one else is doing it, is not a good enough reason. It may well be that no one else is doing it because there are not enough people who want it.

We all have different views in life and we all like and dislike different things. Just because you believe that your idea is unique and 'something special', doesn't mean that others will and never assume others will feel the same way. That is not to say it won't be in hot demand but the most crucial thing to do here, is to do your research.

New ideas are often very hard to get off the ground and the likes of Facebook and Google are exceptions, so why not look at existing markets and find a way of delivering them in a better way?

Whichever route you chose, research will help. Research comes in a variety of formats and each one of them is important.

a) Online research is a must, as it will quickly identify if your product or service exists and whether it's in demand. If there are lots of similar businesses then there is clearly a big demand and that is not necessarily a bad thing. If this is the case, ask yourself; "What can I do better? Why will people buy from me?"

   If the market doesn't exist, try and find out if anyone has tested it before. If they have, why wasn't it successful? Perhaps your idea is slightly different!

b) The second form of research is 'real people'. Ask around, would people buy your idea? Why would or wouldn't they buy? What would they pay? Starting with family and friends is the easiest and quickest way but remember, people close to you either want to encourage you and therefore say what you want to hear, or are jealous or envious and tell you things to discourage you.

   Don't be put off by this, and whatever you do, don't argue with people if they don't like your idea. Remember, we all like different things!

c) If you believe you have a good idea, consider approaching a business mentor or consultant. Don't be put off by the title. Sure, there are business consultants who charge extraordinary high fees but these are generally helping large corporations.

   There are many, who genuinely want to help small business grow and develop and will work with you and help you to achieve your goal.

A number of them, like DAA Consulting, also offer free mentoring for start-ups. They understand that most people starting out in business do not have an endless source of funds.

They will help you obtain finance or to find grants where available, as well as look at your marketing strategy and direct you to the right sources. Some may even defer part of their fees until the business can support itself. It's always worth asking!

They will almost certainly provide you with an initial free consultation and look constructively upon your idea and give you a genuine unbiased opinion. Remember, these are people who have been there, seen it, done it. Whilst no one has a crystal ball, most consultants and advisors will have a pretty good idea of the potential pitfalls your idea may have and how to overcome them.

Identifying pitfalls and problems, should always be taken constructively. By identifying areas of concern, you can look at ways to prevent them from stopping what you want to achieve before it's too late.

So the first steps in starting your business are:

- ✓ *The idea: - Never start a business, for the sake of starting a business!*
- ✓ *Is there a market for the idea? - Has it been tried before?*
- ✓ *Does the market exist? – If so, can you do better?*
- ✓ *Do your research – Online, friends and family, independent business advisors.*

You will also need to work out what type of marketing, pricing and business model will best attract your target customers – more about this later.

Are you Passionate?

People have often approached me and said "*I'd really like to start a business, but I don't know what type of business to start, can you give me some ideas?*" My immediate answer to this is always the same, "*What do you enjoy doing? What interests you?*" "*Is there anything you are passionate about?*"

When starting out, you don't have to be an expert in your field but it does help enormously if you do something that interests or excites you.

This way, you will not only learn fast, but your passion for your product or service will shine through. These two elements go a long way to helping you become successful.

Many successful entrepreneurs say that making money was secondary and that the reason they started their business was their belief that they could offer their customers something better.

Remember: If you don't share in that passion or believe in your idea, why should your customers? The chances are, they won't and your business is more likely to fail.

Business Model

With your idea and research in tow and before starting out on the road to business, you next need to decide which business structure to opt for. You will need to:

- *Choose a trading name for your start up*

- *Decide the way you will trade (sole trader, partnership, limited company)*

- *Think about where you will trade from, and the costs involved*

- *Pick who you will bank with*

- *Notify the relevant authorities you are trading*

Again, research is required to find out what are the pros and cons of the relevant structures in relation to your idea. You could speak to an accountant or, if you decided to consult with an advisor or mentor, the likelihood is that he or she will be able to guide you in the initial stages.

The choice of structure will inform your future growth; therefore, picking the best-suited structure is as imperative as keeping accurate records of your business.

Business Planning

The next step is creating your business plan: this is where you can map out how your business is going to get to where you want it to be in three to five years time.

Without a clear vision, a business is less likely to succeed, yet it is surprising how many people start out without one. Similar to the view that many people have about the advisors, many also think that a business-plan is a daunting and unnecessary.

Simply put, a business plan is purely an amalgamation of your thoughts. You will have already thought why it is that you believe your idea will be a success and why people will want to buy from you. A business plan is a written culmination of those thoughts.

It does however, have two main fundamental advantages:

> Firstly, it focuses your mind on other issues you may not yet have thought of, and as referred to above, it helps you identify how you are going to overcome those pitfalls you previously identified, as well as think about any others. By putting this down on paper, you will have a constant reference to what you have set out to do, to help keep you on track.

> Secondly, a comprehensive plan is needed to persuade other people to provide funding if required. Starting a business will almost certainly need some form of funding, whether it be; a start-up loan, a bank loan, an overdraft or even an investment from a private individual.

Branding

At this point, you need to consider the image of your business; for example the name and logo. These need to stand out and be unique in the increasingly globalised and crowded market. Before starting a business, it's a good idea to incorporate this image on a well designed website, and all this ideally needs to be fully completed before your business goes live.

Not all businesses need a website but most will. Again, discuss this with your advisor. Depending on what your business is, your website could be where most people will come across your business and decide whether to buy your products or services. All very important issues when starting a business.

However, your website is so much more than just a pretty, colourful set of images, graphics and words. If your business is likely to benefit from a website, then it needs to be well presented, easy to read and most crucially, be keyword friendly.

Your website needs to be found. It's pointless having a great looking website if nobody can find it. It's a bit like printing a leaflet or flyer for your business and then keeping it in your draw. It's pointless - it needs to be out there and be seen.

Positioning your website where it can be found i.e. high on the search engines and directories, does not need to be expensive although it can be time consuming.

However, this is where your passion and enthusiasm for your idea can really flourish. Posting blogs, writing articles and joining in conversations online is great for business and the more authoritative you appear, the more people will be drawn to you.

Cash Flow Management

Finally, before starting out, you need to make sure your finances are all in order.

Cashflow is the number one reason why so many businesses fail so quickly and again this is where planning comes in, which will form part of your business plan.

This will mean getting an accounting and cash flow system up and running ASAP, so that you don't get buried in invoices and receipts and lose sight of the viability of your fledgling business.

Even long established businesses can suffer negative cash flow issues and go under if tight controls aren't kept in place. 'Cash is king' in business and it's all too easy to be carried away with sales and not keep a close enough eye on costs.

As previously mentioned, taking advice at an early stage can help enormously, especially when it comes to forecasting and managing cash flow and it is important to remember that 70% of small businesses that receive mentoring survive for five years or more, which is double the rate of those who don't.

TWO - BUSINESS START UP LOANS

As stated in the last chapter, the first steps into business can be both exciting and scary. They can also be the point where many get lost or give up because, whilst the research shows there is a demand, the bank balance may show a lack of funding.

You have the idea, you have the skill, you have the time but do you have the finance?

Not every business will need a loan to start up but if your business plan has demonstrated that it will, don't get confused or overwhelmed with the options with where to begin.

There are a number of traditional choices, such as bank loans and overdrafts as well as new ones such as crowd funding and peer to peer lending.

These last few years have seen a dramatic decline in the traditional forms of funding and the new sources, such as crowd funding often require fairly inspirational or elaborate ideas to be attractive to investors.

One of the easier and speedier formats available today, is the government-backed Start-Up Loan scheme. Not everyone will qualify but again, a business advisor can help discuss your options and help you with the application process.

How do I know if I qualify for a start-up loan?

Last year over 500,000 new businesses registered with Companies House and this number is set to rise. Many started their journey with the help of a business start-up loan and this is set to continue.

The first thing you need to know is that start-up loans are exactly that: for businesses who are starting up! However, businesses younger than 24 months old are also considered to be start-ups and can qualify.

This is great news for those who didn't know about start-up loans or didn't feel they needed one when they originally started their business, so if this is you and you'd like to apply or know more, get in contact.

So, if you're about to launch a business or have been trading for less than two years, you are eligible and could qualify for a start-up loan.

In order to apply, you will need to put in place a business plan. As mentioned in the previous chapter, a business plan is always needed when applying for any form of finance. As also stated, this is something that most entrepreneurs can start by themselves but if they need help, this is available.

START-UP LOANS

The business plan does not need to be overly complicated but it does need to be as precise as possible and realistic. Preparing a plan for a business with no track record can be difficult as financial forecasts, which are an absolute necessity for obtaining any form of loan, are based on assumptions.

However, with the help of an expert who has experienced the ups and downs of business, a number of sensible assumptions can be made.

A business consultant or advisor can be a good place to start in simplifying the process as well as offering expertise where needed and very often an arrangement can be made to defer any costs involved until the loan has been granted.

Why does a start-up need a business plan?

A business plan will help an idea come to life, as it helps to predict figures, set goals and provide an action plan showing how your business will come together.

Businesses as well as lenders need solid figures to work towards and a business plan provides this as well as helping to establish whether an idea has got 'legs'. The plan will need to show that the business can make back the money that it has borrowed as well as operate in profit.

All lenders will insist on a business plan, as it is their only way of understanding your business and what is involved in it.

Engaging with a business advisor will not only help you with formatting a plan, it will also give the lender comfort that your ideas have been overseen by an experienced eye.

How much can I borrow?

Every loan application is different and is considered according to the needs of your business, with an average loan size of around £6,000.

Each owner of the business can apply individually, so as long as the money is used for the business and as long as the business plan identifies the need and is within the maximum limit, then that is the amount that can be applied for.

Applications of between £1,000 and £25,000 per business owner can be submitted, so if there are three owners, then an application of up to £75,000 can be made.

What are the repayment terms?

Typically, the terms of repayment are three to five years, with an interest rate of 6.2%. Loans can sometimes benefit from a capital holiday in the first year, although this is not guaranteed.

Although the loans must be used for the benefit of the business, they are personal loans and each owner who is successfully granted the loan, is personally liable for its repayment in the event that the business does not succeed.

Three - HOW SMALL BUSINESSES BENEFIT FROM MENTORS

Because starting and running a business can be one of the most exciting and stressful times in the life of an entrepreneur, it is often good to have someone to turn to, who understands what you are going through.

Business mentors differ slightly from advisors and consultants, in so much as their main focus is on encouraging and helping you keep your mind on track.

Their job is not to do the work for you but to guide you in the right direction and keep you focused on the issues within your business that can often be overlooked.

This can be anything from concentrating on your niche market, to finance, staffing or marketing but essentially ensuring that your mind remains set on your objections.

Staying on top of things isn't easy. This is where the role of a mentor will come in handy as having someone to talk to who understands your aims, can be invaluable.

What do mentors do for businesses?

A mentor is a seasoned and successful businessperson. Choosing a mentor depends on the needs of the company. Assess your situation.

Are you worried which direction to take? A mentor won't advise you but they will help you think things through with a clear mind. Think about the directions of your business you are unsure of. This will help you:

a) Make the right choice and
b) Get the most out of your mentorship.

Business mentors are on hand to encourage, inspire and motivate. Accountability in business is a great thing to spur entrepreneurs on to meet their goals.

A mentor will sit down with you and look at your business and ideas from an objective perspective. A mentor may question you on these plans, ideas and objectives.

There will be an element of troubleshooting. Be prepared for constructive criticism. Remember that they are there to help you.

Remember also that no business problem is solved, without some sort of strategy.

A mentor will not only help you to come up with that strategy but will also guide you in implementing it but will not do it for you.

A mentor can be a valuable aide in helping keep you on track and steering you back on course should you start to alter but a mentor's job is not to advise you or to do the work for you. This is something for you to do.

They are there however, to encourage you, motivate you and make you think about how you could change, implement and improve things.

Do I need a business mentor?

If you have a seed of an idea but are unsure what you should do next, or are apprehensive about moving forward, you could benefit from a business mentor.

Mentors can play an important role in all businesses, even when they are set up and running smoothly. Mentors don't always come on board at the beginning of a business; they can be appointed at any time, so don't think that by talking with a mentor at the outset is a sign of weakness. It's not!

Working with a mentor can help your business grow and expand. You may have started alone but are now ready to move on to the next stage of growth. Expansion, employment and even implementing new ideas can usually benefit from the help of a mentor who has been there and done it!

What do mentors have to offer?

Working with a business mentor can help you solve all sorts of different problems in your business. It is not uncommon for business owners to get so wrapped up in certain issues that they cannot see the wood for the trees. Business owners often find it difficult to talk to people outside of their business and that's where a business mentor can come in.

A business mentor will look at things objectively, from an independent point of view and often see things that you haven't seen. Maybe you're not sure about some of the logistical day-to-day issues in your business. This is where a mentor can help you, by guiding you and talking it through with you.

Mentors bring years of experience. Something that may look like a major problem to a businessperson who is just starting out may look minor to a mentor who has already been in that situation and overcome it.

Working with a mentor can bring a wealth of knowledge. They will have learnt things that you may need in the future and you can also learn from the mistakes they made in their early days. Any successful entrepreneur will have made a few mistakes along the way and can help prevent you from making the same mistakes.

Successfully working with a mentor

There are a few key habits to practise, when working with a mentor:

- *Be responsive.* A great working relationship will take good communication from both parties. Be respectful of your mentor's time and respond in a timely fashion to their correspondence.

- *Be proactive.* The best results come when you put their advice into action. Never stop generating ideas for your business. Take them to your mentor for feedback. It makes the whole process much more enjoyable and productive.

- *Stay enthusiastic.* It can sometimes be difficult to hear that there are improvements that need to be made in your business but keep the end goal in mind: Success, and remind yourself of your goals.

Famous entrepreneurs and their mentors

As mentioned above, mentors don't just play a role in start-ups. Many successful business owners refer to mentors.

The likes of Bill Gates, Richard Branson and Mark Zuckerburg are all successful business people who count their mentors as integral parts of their personal development and business life.

We all know that no success is made overnight and it is mentors behind-the-scenes that can often see the potential in an individual or a business and help to drive both the business and the individual, forward.

Time to find a mentor?

DAA Consulting offer excellent business mentoring packages, many of which are free and can tremendously benefit people who are thinking of starting their own business.

There is no one-size-fits all approach to business mentoring. Businesses can expect tailored advice, face-to-face meetings and even telephone conferences.

Business mentoring can help business owners find solutions, set attainable goals and create streamlined strategies; with the aim of improving existing businesses and help new businesses reach their full potential in all areas.

Four - TOP TIPS FROM BUSINESS LEADERS

There is no time like the present to begin to shape your business exactly how you want it. Take some tips on board and learn what the best in business are saying.

So, I've rounded up the top tips to get your business in shape, and all inspired by business leaders, some famous and some I've had the privilege to know and work with.

Be charitable

Did you know that customers are likely to buy a product that benefits a great cause?

Aside from the fact that being involved with a charity does something good, it can also establish positive attention for your organisation. It need not be something large scale. If you are a micro business, why not choose a local charity to team up with?

For example, run an event and get your staff involved. Increasing awareness of a good cause *and* gaining sales at the same time is a win-win scenario for both.

Thought inspired by Dan McCabe, Director of SixDegrees.org

Slow down and reassess

Running a business can be hectic. With seemingly hundreds of tasks, it can be easy to get overwhelmed. Make use of time-tracking software such as Toggl to check if you're spending a reasonable time on particular tasks.

Emails, for example, can be a massive time-suck. Are there things that you could outsource, or put to the bottom of your list?

Use 'S.T.O.P' to help you to reassess and get things back in order.

S - slow down
T - take deep breaths
O - observe your tasks
P - proceed

Thought and 'S.T.O.P' inspired by Scott Eblin, author of Overworked and Overwhelmed

Keep an eye on industry trends

Who are the leaders in your industry? Why not follow them on social media?

Set some time aside to catch up on what they're saying. Are there any key dates that you should observe, or industry events that you could attend?

Keep an ear to the ground for conversations that may shake up the way you offer your service and sell your product. Deloitte, Accenture and others offer insightful industry reports for varying sectors.

Get a mentor

It can be difficult to navigate the world of business but there's no reason to be alone. The internet has a wealth of resources but there is nothing like one-to-one coaching. This is where a mentor can come in. They offer tailored advice and guidance.

Look for a mentor who is seasoned and successful in business, who is willing to spend time helping you and your business to develop. (If you need a business mentor you know who you can talk to!)

Thought inspired by Richard Branson in his Guide to finding a Mentor.

Embrace cloud technology

The digital age has done businesses major favours.

Whilst sometimes there is nothing quite like a face-to-face meeting, cloud software is making it easier than ever to add a whole new dynamic to the way your company works. Having all of your documents and correspondence on one handy system makes remote working easier than ever. Your location will no longer be a hindrance, as long as you have a Wi-Fi connection.

Business moves fast. Your diary can be synced with that of your clients and colleagues. That doc that needs updating?......Why not do it on the move?

Cloud technology is here to stay. If you haven't embraced it already, now is the time.

Thought inspired by Jason Richelson, founder and CEO of ShopKeep POS

Invest in yourself

That conference you want to go to? Those books that you haven't yet got round to reading? The news you haven't caught up on?

Create the budget and the time for them. Is there a course or qualification that would help you to excel and become more of an expert in your field? Make this year the year that you accomplish those goals and set yourself the targets. Maybe it will cost you along the way but some of the biggest success stories, come from those that have had to invest in themselves along the way.

It may be as simple as reading a book every month but no harm can come from spending the time to learn from people who are ahead of you.

Thought inspired by Mark Suster, a 2x entrepreneur turned VC.

Remember your purpose

Stopping to refocus every so often and look at the reason you started out on your business journey is a fantastic way to keep you on track.

If what you are doing does not match up with your objectives, look at tweaking your strategy and doing things differently. That way, when it gets tough, you can remind yourself of your 'why'.

Every great company has a 'why'. Write down your mission statement and put it somewhere visible. It will give you and your team something to work towards.

Do you have a team? Make sure that they are working towards the same thing as you. Set the culture of your business and make sure it's enforced every time someone new comes along. Communicating it internally means that your customers and clients will quickly grasp it too.

Five – WHAT IS A BUSINESS ANALYSIS AND DO I NEED ONE?

So you've had your idea, researched it, identified your needs, written your business plan, put your finances in place and started your business.

So why do I now need a review? Firstly, it's always good to keep an eye on your original plan and constantly review it. Very often a business analysis or review is carried out several years down the line when the business has veered off track and is doing something very different to its original plan.

By then, profits may not be as strong as you'd like, costs may be higher than they should be and staff may be more troublesome or demoralized than expected. At the same time, sales have stagnated and the whole business has become complacent.

It's at that this stage that a business owner looks back and wonders why they have allowed it to fall behind so much and moan and whine using the phrase 'in-hindsight' or if-only'. Well it doesn't have to be like that!

We talked above about the need for a business plan. The plan was there for a reason: To establish the principles of your business and set goals and aims. But day-to-day managing and running of the business has meant that the plan hasn't been looked at since it was initially used to get that loan, right at the start!

So why wait for the business to self-steer itself off-track? It may or may not be on a collision course but the chances are that it's not on the same course it first set itself on. That's not to say that plans don't change, sometimes they do, but have they changed for the right reason?

It may have been a strategic decision to change but the chances are that it has changed because nobody has been keeping it on the right course!

Many good ideas or strategies that were originally thought of in that first plan may have been forgotten or overlooked. Keeping a constant eye on the original plan is a valuable commodity. After all, that was how you saw the business succeeding in the first place. Therefore, having a regular review is vital and should be encouraged.

There can be many costs involved in creating, running and maintaining your business. With so much involvement in the day-to-day upkeep, it can be difficult to see how you can run things more smoothly or improve your operations. This is where a business analysis or review comes in and can be best seen by someone with a fresh pair of eyes.

What is a business analysis?

A business analysis or review is a specific set of activities, which allows business owners and stakeholders to look objectively at the needs of an organisation, its problems and most importantly, to find solutions for them.

If done regularly, it is really no more than a review of what the business plans were and whether they have been implemented. There is nothing wrong with updating and amending a plan. After all, when it was first written, it was done with a lot less insight.

A business analysis examines the processes of a business and sets about implementing change that will streamline the infrastructure of a company. In turn, this will add value to a company, as they change processes that are not working and analyse ways that work can be done more effectively.

By analysing the current needs of the business whilst reviewing its previous plan, a strategic course can be maintained. When the original plan was introduced, it was prepared with limited knowledge but as the business developed, lessons have been learned and a regular review can keep the business remain on a firm footing.

Do only large businesses need business analysis?

It is a myth that only large businesses can make use of a business analyst. Whether it is a government organisation, not-for-profit or a for-profit business, large or small, all will benefit from the work of a business analyst.

No matter the size, every business needs to regularly analyse and review its position and re-assess its strategy and plans.

For a very large organisation, an in-house business analyst may be more useful, as the company operates on a larger scale in terms of turnover, project scope, clients and finance but for a smaller business, either the owner or a business advisor can do it, either individually or hand in hand.

Can't I just be my own business analyst?

Yes, to a degree. However a business analysis is often best performed by an outside individual. Why? Because an outside analyst:

- **Has an expert set of skills**

- **Can view your business objectively, from an unbiased perspective**

- **Leaves you free to begin to implement change.**

I can't afford a business analyst

It is an even bigger myth that a business analysis must be a costly process. In fact, you can often obtain a free review of your business from an expert. DAA Consulting offer a free initial review and your report will provide you with insight into vital changes that can be implemented quickly. These can show where you may have strayed from the initial vision and mission of your business.

The choice to then invest into a more in-depth business analysis or engage with DAA Consulting in implementing change is completely left to you.

Six - 6 Things That Make A Startup Thrive

Do you ever find that when you finally figure out a simple solution to a big problem, you think: *"Why didn't anyone tell me that before?"* Or when someone else solves the simple solution for you, you say: *"Why didn't I think of that?"*

It's the same as when you're setting out on the journey of your startup. We all said and felt the same things and so on that note, I wondered what tips some of our own business advisors would have liked to have been given, when they started out.

So here are their answers: Use these tips to stand out from the crowd and allow your business to thrive!

Under-promise and over-deliver

Promising to do too much at once is a sure-fire way to lose the trust and respect of customers and clients. You're much better off at developing an agile way of working, in which you deliver in phases.

The quality of what you deliver should always be better than satisfactory, so that your client knows they can come back to you again and again.

Find a good sounding board outside the business

Some of the best business owners are also some of the best listeners, and you should never be above seeking advice.

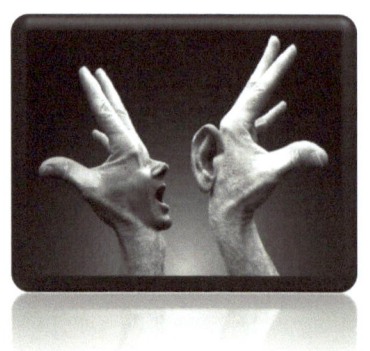

Think about how refreshing it is when you've solved a problem by stepping away from it and coming back to it with a new set of eyes.

By presenting your issues to someone completely unassociated with your business, you can often open yourself up to new ideas.

It gets lonely at the top, so developing a close circle of people whose business acumen you can trust or gaining support from a business consultant, can be a vital asset.

Invest in training and skills development

A great idea is nothing but a great idea, and that doesn't make a great company. To get your business off the ground, you will need solid foundations.

Although training will vary between industries, there are some areas that almost all startup CEO's should train in. Examples include systems-based thinking, managing yourself and driving execution. In short: how to make your dream a reality.

Management and leadership of staff is a key must in today's business world.

Focus on you customer's success

Have you done your research? No, we mean **really** done your research? Because there is little point in trying to combat the market if you don't understand the sector you're going in to.

There are lots of questions to ask before you start selling your idea, but many of them can be answered by looking at the ways in which your customer succeeds.

The more you can help show customers how they can succeed with your product or service, the more closely your can associate your brand with happy customers.

Don't sell the features of your product or service: **sell its benefits**. This, in turn, builds your reputation as an essential vendor and gives your customers, solutions.

Lead with reason, not reaction

It's naturally important to express passion for your business - After all, you started it, it feels like your child! Yet this is often where entrepreneurs go wrong and lead with their emotions instead.

Any decision you make should be made with data and understanding. To achieve this difficult balance you can utilise technology to provide performance analytics, this way you can measure your pre-determined goals.

Once you're used to making fact-based decisions, you'll be able to better understand what works (or doesn't!) and as importantly, why. You can then take corrective action.

Don't be afraid to fall

Dwelling on past failures - or the possibility of failure again - will only stop you moving on to bigger and better things. The important part of failure is assessing what went wrong and learning from it.

The most important part when it comes to failure, however, is balancing your conviction with outside input.

People may tell you that you are going to fail, they are not necessarily correct, but you need to know when you might need some input and suggestions from somewhere else. Everyone has a different viewpoint and what may appear as a winner to some may appear differently to others.

It's always good to listen and then make a judgment call not just at the start of your journey but at all times during your involvement in the world of business, so always be prepared to learn from others.

Seven - 7 Ways To Promote Your Small Business That You Haven't Tried Yet

According to the Global Entrepreneurship Index, the world hit 52% of its entrepreneurial capacity in 2014. This is the delicate ecosystem of small businesses that continues to grow and thrive every single year.

What does this mean for your small business?

In terms of getting noticed, standing out from the crowd may become an increasingly difficult challenge. But, this doesn't mean that it's impossible.

As an entrepreneur you are creative. Here are some ideas of how to promote your small business that you probably haven't tried yet but there are always others.

All you have to do is give each idea a personal touch!

Online demos is one:

Whilst your budget may not stretch to the thousands of pounds that paid-for television and radio advertising costs, the internet has made it possible or start-ups to promote their business to a wide audience for a fraction of the price.

Having a company-specific YouTube channel is a really good step for digital marketing - especially if it's linked up to your Google+ page too. However the real challenge is creating engaging content that your viewers will want to see.

The great thing is, it costs nothing to upload a video but the return could be phenomenal if your video went viral, potentially reaching millions of people worldwide.

Embrace the freebie is another:

The lure of a 'free gift' is often enough to peak peoples' interests, as well as getting your brand noticed. Even better is that gifts don't need to be extravagant. In fact, your brand is more likely to be remembered if the gift is funny, rather than expensive.

Gifts can also come in the form of 'sharing your knowledge!' Free workshops and seminars can be extremely useful and can make your reputation within the industry, extremely authoritative. Giveaways - both items and knowledge - can be given online to keep costs down.

Become a blogger:

If blogging isn't already part of your digital marketing strategy, then the chances are you've been missing a trick. Whilst this concept isn't brand new, it's amazing how many business owners do not use this handy medium. It's often the case that startups don't have the time or resources to keep up with a regular blog but you can employ ad-hoc freelance people.

I have met many small business owners who quite willingly talk with great authority about their industry when visiting friends and colleagues in a social environment but shy away from producing an article online. Fundamentally there is no difference, yet many business owners do not appreciate or understand the importance of blogging.

However, with search engine rankings at stake, as well as promoting your wider brand, a company blog is worth the time and effort that it takes. Combined with a well-implemented social media strategy, the leads will start to roll in.

It's a fundamental fact, that most people would chose to buy from someone they feel is an authority in a particular field, than someone who has simply tried to sell to them. Blogging helps you build an audience without a direct sales approach.

Offer a holistic package:

Do you know of a non-competing business whose ethos fits yours? Teaming up to offer a package deal for both of you could give an edge against your competitors.

Customers love to feel as if they are getting value for money. If a combined package makes it easier for them to get to their final destination with less effort, there will almost surely be an interest and a win-win for all concerned.

For you, this means you will have access to a new stream of customers, who have seen you as a result of an endorsement from someone they already know and trust. It will also provide connections you would not normally get, whilst possibly getting one-up on the competition.

Be the awards:

It goes without saying, that winning an award is both satisfying and extremely rewarding and you would always want your business to win industry awards, but have you ever considered sponsoring them?

Annual award shows give you the opportunity to get your brand out there by becoming a sponsor, as well as networking with the wider industry. Plus these events regularly gain column inches, so you'll be picking up free publicity too!

An added bonus is that by associating your name with well-known awards, you automatically become a trusted name for the customer. This will make you stand out from the crowd and again, give you more authority.

Use smartphone technology:

In 2014, app analytics provider Flurry reported that app usage on smartphones continued to grow, to the detriment of mobile web.

With this in mind, if your business would lend itself to an app platform, why not invest in the development of one? Like most new and innovative products, prices fall over time and whilst a couple of years ago, apps were generally price prohibitive for small businesses, technology is changing and prices have become more competitive.

Incorporate buzzwords:

Embracing both current trends and popular culture could be the way your company breaks through a marketing dead-end. This means looking outside your own industry and doing some research into what is going on in the wider world.

I'm sure you have heard of a selfie? But have you heard about the latest superfood? Getting the lowdown on what is trending could earn you serious points with potential customers. I'm not suggesting that you start taking selfie's or sell the latest superfoods but look at these and other buzzwords as marketing tools for your business.

These are just a few ways you can get started with alternative marketing strategies. People like trendy things and if you are seen as a 'modern' business that embraces modern ways, people will be more attracted to you.

All it really takes is a little inspiration and some thinking from out of the box to come up with new and innovative ways to get the word out about your business and what you have to offer.

The real importance comes with injecting the same passion you have for your business into your marketing. For more information on how to translate that into progress, get in touch with one of our business consultants and we'd be happy to help.

Eight - START FOLLOWING AND GET FOLLOWED!

As a business owner, you have probably heard the words 'digital marketing' and 'social media marketing' thrown around.

The importance of getting your brand out on the internet is key to any business growth, but really all you need to know is how using Social Media can get you more referrals, leads and in the end, how it can get you more customers?

Photo: GoAwesomeness

I'm going to explain why using Social Media is so integral to your marketing strategy and also offer you tips on how to make Twitter work especially well for your small or medium business.

Looking back to move forward

A mere 20 years ago, your loyal customers would be built through word-of-mouth recommendations, or a well-crafted advert placed in the local newspaper.

As time moved on technology advanced, bringing with it new marketing methods such as direct mail, telemarketing and trade shows. These were very successful, and still can be today, but as consumer's became wise to these methods they also became very good at avoiding traditional attempts to get their attention.

Today, social media and the use of digital marketing is the way that small businesses get noticed online.

We can't escape social media, it is everywhere, so ignoring the rise and rise of this form of communication would be a big mistake for any business. As the old saying goes: if you can't beat them, join them!

Connecting with customers

Never before has there been a more immediate and intimate way to connect with customers, especially when you consider that 62% of adults worldwide use some form of social media.

This can be through computers, smartphones, tablets, games consoles and more.

Take, for example, these extremely impressive statistics:

- One billion people actively use Facebook every month
- 500,000 people use Twitter every month
- Google's +1 button is used 2+ billion times each day
- 5 million photos are uploaded to Instagram every hour
- 3,600 hours of video are uploaded to YouTube every hour

So, if you're not already tapping into this goldmine of marketing opportunities by utilising social media, you could be doing your business out of gaining new customers every day.

If this is you, don't worry, we've got the tips you need to get you started on social media, and in particular, Twitter today.

Why Twitter?

Whilst having a social media strategy that extends over many platforms such as Facebook, YouTube, Google+ and Instagram is a brilliant idea, Twitter is the ideal place to start out.

No other medium gets you inside a business or brand quite like Twitter. This is because rather than potential customers seeking out your specific business, you may be found simply because somebody searched for '#smallbusiness' or '#personalassistant' or '#london'.

This instant accessibility, without the need for adding connections, or approving posts, makes Twitter the perfect practice ground for your social media strategy.

How to get started

Firstly, before you've even created a Twitter account, remember to **stay brand loyal.** You may be Joe Bloggs, CEO of Bloggs Paper Inc, but nobody else knows that. Therefore, your Twitter handle shouldn't be @JoeBloggs, but instead @BloggsPaperInc - remember you are tweeting as the business, not as yourself.

Likewise, the profile photo should reflect the business, and ideally the business logo, not yourself. Again, it is the business you are promoting.

Now that you're all set up, it's time to **complete your profile.** Each section of your Twitter profile can give potential leads more detail about your business, so making sure you fill in the location website and bio is principal.

Then it's time to start **following people!** It's all very exciting but you need to take it slow because Twitter has strict rules about what they call 'aggressive following'.

But, in general, you should start by following those in the following categories:

- Your customers;
- Your business partners;
- Your competitors or peers;
- Your trade or professional organisations;
- Your customers;
- Your business partners;
- Your competitors or peers;
- Businesses in your neighbourhood;
- Businesses run by people you know.

Twitter can actually help with these initial stages by scanning your address book to see who you know, is already on Twitter.

Finally, you can start **interacting with Tweeters.** Exactly what you want to tweet about, will be unique to your business and your business alone but in general you will want to find a balance between interesting things that engage your audience, whilst at the same time, promoting your business.

Whatever you do though, make sure that you give out useful information about things in general. Don't sell yourself but offer opinions on things in general.

There is no problem with telling people about offers you have but don't keep telling them. Instead engage with them, just as you would if you were talking to them face to face. People will un-follow you if they feel they are just being sold to.

Always answer any questions you might get, as this is how you will begin to become a valuable member of the community. Becoming a valuable member is important, it's just the same as being a member of a club.

Over to you

Naturally, these are just suggestions and the direction your digital marketing takes you, could differ greatly. Even if you decide to outsource this, don't loose sight of what is being tweeted and never feel you can't add your own tweet whenever you feel you have something to add.

Once you have Twitter under your belt, you can expand on how you are interacting on social media in a vast variety of ways, including using other media and actively driving traffic to your website or blog.

Nine – WATCHING THE COSTS IN YOUR NEW BUSINESS

Part of the reason why starting up a business can be very challenging is because of cash flow, as mentioned in chapter one. Part of the planning and preparation is to make sure that you are financially sound. Whether you are taking out a start-up loan or financing the business yourself, it is vital to keep costs to a minimum, wherever possible and in the most cost effective ways.

Shop Around

You should do this often. This is not just about bartering and trying to get things on the cheap but about looking at what you need in the way that you need it.

When you are buying equipment, don't be too hasty to purchase everything brand new. It really does pay to shop around. Think of exactly what you need everything for. Will a refurbished computer do the same job as a brand new one? Chances are, it will.

The same can apply to things like business insurance. When you're shopping around, compare the best-tailored quotes. It's convenient to do everything online but never underestimate the benefit of negotiating with someone on the phone. Also, many online services are great for consumers but not always so good for small businesses.

Often, a personal relationship in business with a broker or supplier is invaluable which you can't usually get online.

Don't forget also, there are a number of business banking options on the market, for new businesses. It is not uncommon for banks to offer businesses free banking or reduced fees, during the company's early stages.

Seek those deals out and make the most of them but don't forget to re-examine them when the deal comes to an end.

Outsource

There will come a point where you may need a PA, a graphic designer or a copywriter but can you afford them all at once? Maybe you can but is it *smart?* This is where outsourcing works well.

Making good use of cloud storage can also be beneficial and save you money on software. With free programmes like Google Drive, Evernote and Skype, running your business can be made easier than ever by getting much of the work you need done, without always employing people full time.

Get Great Advice

Without a professional casting their eye over your business plan, it can often be difficult to see where you could make better savings.

A business analyst is the ideal individual to advise you, from an objective standpoint. They will look at your plans, suggest improvements and improve your strategy. You will inevitably reduce costs, seeing the benefits in the short and long term.

Ten - WHAT ATTRACTS A TALENTED EMPLOYEE TO AN SME?

Now, you may wonder why we want to talk about this in this guide. After all, this guide is aimed at helping people understand what is involved in starting and running a small business. Well, if you are going to look at employing people, you need to understand things from an employee's point of view too.

Whether you're a new business, or an established SME, getting you hands on new talent can prove difficult. This is especially true for those with a specialised skill who may already be in a secure position.

Without the support of a generously funded HR department, you might find it hard to get the message out there about why a prospective employee should work for you, so it is very important that you emphasis the successes of the SME and figure out exactly what aspects will appeal to prospective employees.

Not too sure? Well, we've put together a handy guide for you!

A recent study carried out by <u>Nescafe Alegria and YouGov</u> has shown that the key benefits of working in an SME are;

i)   A friendly atmosphere,
ii)   Having a close relationship with colleagues and bosses, and
iii)   Having a say in the future of the company

So now, we are going to reveal exactly what it is that employees love so much about SMEs and how you can use that to nab the best talent there is on the market. I have picked a number of key objectives and looked at the stats surrounding those objectives and then looked at what you can do to get the most out of them.

Friendly colleagues

The stats: Most important for employees and employers alike was providing a positive work environment, with a majority saying that this was a key advantage to working in a SME as opposed to a larger company.

What you can do: The best way to ensure your working environment remains positive, is to have open lines of communication. SME's have the advantage here, as they are typically less bureaucratic, so there are normally closer relationships between the leadership and the employees.

Building relationships

The stats: Another big hitter on why people chose to work for a small company was the ability to get to know more of the employees. Almost half (49%) of 18 - 24 year old employees polled felt that they have a better social life with their colleagues in an SME than in a larger business or corporate.

In fact, working relationships developed a bit of a theme as 45% of SME employees said that having a closer relationship with their manager made them happier at work.

What you can do: Treat your business philosophy like an extension of your family. By dong this, your workforce and employees will feel more included and appreciated.

Treasured opinions

The stats: Being able to offer input into the future of the company was seen as an advantage. However, employers found this more valuable than employees, with 61% of the former to 41% of the latter.

What you can do: This shows that although employees feel like they have more of a say with an SME, employers could work a little harder on making sure their employees critique is taken on board.

Flexible working hours

Photo: Pixabay

The stats: Both employers and employees agree that flexible working hours make employees happy.

What you can do: SMEs are much more likely to be able to tailor a job to deal with employees' individual needs.

For example, if Monday is the only day an employee can't get childcare, a small business may be more willing than a big company to allow that employee to work from home one day a week.

Progression

The stats: Unfortunately, this is one of the areas where SME's fall down. Many employees feel like they won't be able to climb the career ladder so quickly, or move on to dizzier heights, when working for an SME.

What you can do: With a smaller workforce, it's true that there may be less opportunities. However, on the other hand, the role you can offer a potential employee, in many cases is more varied and has more breadth than at a big company, where employees tend to specialise more.

In addition, loyalty means much more to an SME, so when high growth happens, your best employees should be the first in line for a reward!

Their success is your success

It's an oft-cited cliché, but the success of any business really is down to its employees, so getting the pick of the crop is in your best interests. But don't stress about how to get the best candidates, instead focus on selling your winning business culture and people will soon realise why yours is a great place to work.

Eleven - 11 TOP BLOGS FOR STARTUPS TO FOLLOW

With the sheer amount of entrepreneurial spirit around, it's not a surprise that there is no shortage of blogs that aim to help startups get off the ground. This could be anything from gaining insight from entrepreneurs themselves, to more general information from other industries.

Either way, we have put together a list of blogs which are well worth following and given you an example article for each one:

Quora

Quora is one of the best resources online for small business owners, entrepreneurs and startups. This Q&A site lets you gain access to experts who take the time to give you a serious answer to your question.

You can follow particular topics that you may be interested in, for example 'digital marketing', or certain inspirational people, such as Mark Zuckerberg.

Example article: Small business: What is the best e-commerce solution for a small business?

Entrepreneur

Entrepreneur covers pretty much every aspect of starting up and running small businesses, from case studies to top tips.

You can learn from the successes and failures of others, and with updates added every day the site is never short on content.

Example article: The 3 Things You Need to Know About Hiring a Social Media Manager

CopyBlogger

If you want to learn how to improve your content marketing, CopyBlogger is the place that can teach you how to create engaging content.

You can use this advice across all of your customer communication, whether that be social media, blogs, email marketing or just anything else.

Example article: How to learn from your successes

Wise Bread

If financial advice is what you're after, WiseBread offers advice from a collection of writers on saving money, cutting costs and implementing good budgets.

Money can often be very tight as a small business owner, so tips on business finances should always be appreciated and thought about.

Example article: 7 Times Buying Generic Will Cost You

CoDrops

Chances are that if you're running a startup, you're doing a bit of everything. Even if you're not directly doing the web design for your business, you'll be overseeing it, so keeping up with the latest web design trends on CoDrops is a grand idea.

Keep up with the ever-evolving look of web design, grab some new ideas or just get inspired!

Example article: Techniques for Creating Textured Text

Search Engine Journal

With contributions from various SEO professionals, you'll find SEO-relevant news, SEO tools, tips and reviews on SEJ.

SEJ particularly focusses on building quality links instead of spam linking.

Example article: 6 Ways To Keep Your Readers Coming Back For More Content

Small Business Brief

Listed as a Forbes Favorite back in 2010, Small Business Brief is still going strong in 2015. Listing small business news, views and reviews, this blog can also give you an insight into the world of other successful entrepreneurs.

Forbes.com reports: "Small Business Brief" is like reading a thick business magazine, loaded with the kind of articles you'd ordinarily earmark and highlight."

Example article: Short Term Thinking Can Harm Your Business

Duct Tape Marketing

Run by John Jantsch, a marketing and digital technology coach, Duct Tape Marketing focusses on small business marketing on a budget.

From social media, to good ole fashioned word-of-mouth, Jantsch gives advice with frugality at the forefront of his mind.

Example article: How to Make Your Brand Matter

The Entrepreneurial Mind

If you were good at paying attention in class, this may be the best way for you to learn all about your startup.

Written by Jeff Cornwall, Chair of Entrepreneurship at Belmont University, The Entrepreneurial Mind offers business advice from someone who teaches it for a living.

Example article: Finding a Niche in a Mature Industry

Business Insider

With exclusive interviews, how-to guides and business tips, Business Insider offers four main categories to keep you in the loop; tech, finance, politics and strategy.

Check in here for all things business and entrepreneurial.

Example article: People decide if you're successful within 5 seconds of meeting you — here's how to look the part

And, of course, you'll want to stay up to date with the DAA Consulting blog.

Here is where you can find all things startup. We can offer you tips, tricks and advice, especially for startups and small businesses in Hertfordshire and beyond!

Example article: A getting-started guide to Twitter for small and medium business

Keeping up to date with the latest goings-on in your industry is essential for small business and startup success. You can get a lot out of reading about the experiences of others and the lessons they have picked up along the way.

If you've found a technique or trick you'd like to try out, we can help guide you in the right direction, or maybe you're looking to start your own business blog. Either way, give us a shout at DAA Consulting and we'll help you get there.

Twelve - THE SECRETS OF WORKING SUCCESSFULLY WITH A BUSINESS PARTNER

There are lots of different factors that make a small business successful. From a practical point of view, you need to have the right legal structure in place, as well as having your accounts and infrastructure in order.

Small businesses should always focus on doing brilliant work, rather than going after the big bucks or worrying solely about making money. If you work on providing the best service or product and looking after your customers, success will come, and as long as small business owners follow their instincts, believe in what they are doing and are passionate about getting it right, customers will keep coming back.

But, if you work with a business partner, it won't matter if you stick to all those rules unless you both believe in the same thing and both have a positive working relationship. Having a business partner in a small business can be a make-or-break situation, so learning how to work together productively and efficiently is key.

Creating a leadership team

Regarded as one of the most valuable traits of any successful business, it is ironic that having a good business partnership is often forgotten about when giving tips on how to run a small business.

Many of the best businesses have begun with two partners and a shared vision:

Google's Larry Page and Sergey Brin, Apple's Steve Wozniak and Steve Jobs, or Hewlett Packard's Bill Hewlett and David Packard, are just a few examples.

It could be time to stop focussing on the success of one individual and instead look to the duo for inspiration!

Take a look at our tips below to find out how to find small business success with a business partner.

Focus on a balancing act

We all have our strengths and weaknesses, but what if we could use the strengths and weaknesses of someone else to complement these? With a business partner, that's exactly what you can do.

Maybe you're not so good at accountancy but have a knack for marketing, but your business partner could be a numbers genius!

Finding the strength in your partner's unique skills will drive your business forward at double speed, as you recognize the differences between the two of you and regard them as assets rather than as faults.

Draw the battle lines

Running a business can sometimes feel like going into a battle, or on occasion, a full-on war! This is why top-performing firms find that a clear division of labour works best to tackle each day's events; it really is divide and conquer!

If you and your business partner have clear, defined roles, you will find that your individual skills, helps your business tick over nicely. More than this, you'll find that unnecessary communication is reduced and time is saved!

This works even better when you are able to divide work according to each of your talents and interests. However, be careful that this does not result in one person thinking that their responsibilities are more important than the other; it really is a balancing act and all roles are just as integral as each other.

Received, loud and clear

Think you're good at communicating? You may be a pro at getting your ideas across in a clear and concise manner, but how good are you at receiving other people's messages? With a partner, you both need to be good listeners.

Having work acknowledged is imperative in encouraging productivity, so even if you disagree with your business partner, make sure you are taking their suggestions on board and working together towards a solution, this will save time in the long run.

You scratch my back...

This initially sounds so obvious, but can get lost along the way: the arrangement between business partners should be beneficial for both parties! As long as the relationship is mutually beneficial, there shouldn't be any question over whether it is worthwhile or not.

It's ok to walk away

Sometimes, it doesn't work out, and that's ok. If a business relationship is no longer working, it's often more productive for both sides to end the partnership amicably and refocus their attention elsewhere, than to try and force something that isn't working. And who knows, you may end up working together in the future!

Always keep an eye open for this scenario. It is too dangerous to allow a situation to continue if one side is no longer happy with the arrangement.

Business partnerships are like a marriage and disagreements can easily occur.

As soon as the first signs appear, it's important that you not only recognize it but that you address it, before it's too late.

Disputes are costly, not only financially but also to the damage that can be caused to the business whilst the dispute is going on.

There are plenty of other practices, which make business partnerships work, but these few are a good place to start and we'd recommend keeping them in mind. Of course, partnerships aren't for everyone, plenty of people go it alone and are just as successful, but having a partner can help in many ways.

Therefore, make sure you assess your individual situation and take a step back before you take the plunge. Sometimes it makes sense and sometimes it doesn't! Think hard and again, look at taking advice.

Thirteen - SMALL BUSINESS BRANDING AND THE IMPORTANCE OF THE LOGO

Large companies world-wide, know and understand how important branding is.

It has long been recognised that having a solid brand brings plenty of value.

But to many small business owners, the time taken to implement a quality visual identity would drain too many financial resources and take away valuable time too.

But even with a limited budget, small and medium businesses can benefit from the impact of a well-honed image, because at the very base of the issue, a brand image can allow an SME to stand apart from the competitors.

Typically, branding may be very expensive, but there are various options available to entrepreneurs to decrease the cost, including outsourcing your design work to a trusted freelancer.

So, we've put together the following tips to help you build a powerful brand image, without breaking the bank.

Keep it simple

Not only does keeping your logo simple make it easier for customers to look at and remember, but keeping it minimalistic may also take the price of design down too.

"A good way to think about simplicity is to see how many moving pieces there are in the logo," - Jonah Berger, author of *Contagious: Why Things Catch On.*

Get social

As already mentioned, every business needs to have a social media presence these days, but there's a difference between just having a profile and really utilising it for marketing purposes.

You really want to be consistently engaging with your followers to push your brand identity.

Brand consistency

Your logo tells your customers so much about your brand, so you want to make sure that it's design fits your company's overall message.

Take, for example, the Apple logo. As one of the world's most futuristic corporations, it makes sense that their logo is sleek, and clean and did you realise there is a reason why it is shaped like it is? Part of the apple has a bite in it!

Think of your brand as a person

As a person, you're made up of beliefs, values and purposes, which drive your everyday life. When building your brand, it's vital that you think of this in the same way. Our personality determines how we react to situations and this is what your brand identity should do too.

Aim for remarkability

What is remarkability?

This is when the design is 'worthy of remark' and cuts through everything else to reach your customer. You need a logo, which is relevant, eye-catching and memorable.

Don't try to mimic big brands

Carving your own distinctive identity doesn't only make you look more professional and unique, but it has longevity. Imagine in a few years time you hit the big time, having a brand which is very similar to an already-established company could force you into rebranding, therefore destroying all of your hard work.

Test your market

Trusting your gut isn't necessarily a bad thing, but when it's an important issue like branding, market research is the way to truly find out whether you are heading in the right direction.

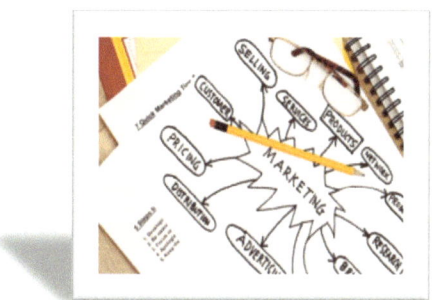

Get some independent feedback from a variety of people about whether your logo is saying what you want it to say then make the appropriate adjustments.

Marketing your brand in new ways

In the past, stamping your logo on everything was good enough to get the word out there, but nowadays this just won't cut it. Respect your customer's intelligence and think of new and innovative ways to get your brand identity recognised.

Think flash mobs (if done correctly, in a fun way), social media and viral videos can be great ways to get your brand out there without appearing as if you are ramming your brand down peoples' throats. It's a great form of indirect selling.

This will generate some intrigue and inspire people to look further into what you have to offer.

Trying to develop your business branding on your own may seem like the ideal way to avoid expensive work. Rather than going to a design firm, you could consider smaller, independent designers who charge much less.

According to Stan Evenson, founder of Evenson Design Group, *"Entrepreneurs on a tight budget should shop around for a designer, but don't hire someone because of their bargain price".*

Find a designer who's familiar with your field and your competition so that they understand your market.

"If the cost still seems exorbitant" Says Stan *"Remember that a good logo should last at least ten years. If you look at the amortization of that cost over a ten-year period, it doesn't seem so bad."*

You may already know what it is you want, and that's a brilliant start, and by consulting with a professional designer who could help you hone your vision as well as give you practical advice such as whether the logo would transfer well into print, can be a solid investment in your business and should not be overlooked.

Your logo is the basis of your brand, as well as the foundation for all your promotional material, so it's one area where spending a little money now can pay off in the long run! It is also something that you should always be proud of.

"It's unwise to pay too much, but it's worse to pay too little.

When you pay too much, you lose a little money - that's all.

When you pay too little, you sometimes lose everything, because the thing you bought was incapable of doing the thing it was bought to do.

The common law of business balance prohibits paying a little and getting a lot - it can't be done".

— <u>John Ruskin</u>

Fourteen - GENERAL ELECTIONS: WHAT THEY MEAN FOR SMALL BUSINESS

At the time of writing, the 2015 UK General Election is just over 20 days away and by the time you've read this, a decision about who should run our country will have been made. It will be interesting to see what changes will be made.

People all over the country are trying to decide who is worthy of their cross on the ballot paper, and this goes for small business owners and startups too. So whether it is this election or the next, or even a bi-election in your local area, you need to consider what affect elections will have on you, as a business owner.

Bearing in mind that one third of the private sector turnover comes from small business, it's no surprise that the main parties are starting to look at getting small business owners on side.

There are various pressure points that political parties can address which concern small business, such as business rates, the cutting of red tape, or regional development plans and programs.

In this section, we look at what is important to you in an election, and what issues can affect your business. We give you the run down on what the main political parties are saying in 2015.

Red Tape

Whether they like it or not, all small business entrepreneurs have to deal with business regulations. At the beginning of this current Parliament, Prime Minister David Cameron promised help for small business, and this came in the form of a three-year initiative to cut red tape.

However a recent study by business information group Croner found that 41% were unsure on the effect that the campaign has had.

For 2015, the two coalition partners have been clear that they want to cut red tape, with the Conservatives shouting a little louder, saying that small business is "disproportionately affected by regulation".

The Liberal Democrats have come out to say that they will establish a Regulation Advisory Board, which will focus on low carbon and efficient innovation. Labour have said, that they would model a US agency set up to assist entrepreneurs and small business, calling it a Small Business Administration.

Business Rates

Business rates can hit you hard wherever you are, and many business owners feel that they are like a hidden tax. This is why there have been repeated calls for changes to the system which governs rates.

Last Autumn, the chancellor George Osborne promised a review on the rates system, and since then has said that rate relief has been doubled until April 2016.

Labour have committed themselves to cutting business rates in 2015, plus they say, 1.5 million business properties could benefit from a freezing of rates in 2016.

The Liberal Democrats meanwhile have said that they will review business rates, which are a "disproportionate burden" on small businesses, and look at alternatives. "*The review will cover the option of moving to site value rating within five years, and in the longer term land value taxation more broadly,*" a spokesman said.

Regional Development

It can feel like a struggle for businesses to get off the ground, but the Liberal Democrats have committed to investing in manufacturing in areas such as motor vehicles, aerospace, low-carbon energy and chemicals to increase international trade by continuing the Regional Growth Fund.

On the other hand, Labour has committed to creating a British Investment Bank and a series of regional banks to boost lending to small businesses.

The Conservatives are looking to transfer power and budgets to cities in the North and like their coalition partners, boast the Regional Growth Fund as an achievement.

The others

Besides the big three, Ukip are determined to exit Europe, and the free trade agreements that go with it. However they assure business owners that cutting bureaucracy will allow them to continue to support businesses in the long run.

On the other side of the spectrum, the Greens are looking to up the minimum wage but they also have a number of small business specific policies such as introducing legislation on late payment and simplifying PAYE.

The Political Playing Field

Despite small business interest in these three areas, it seems that UK businesses aren't panicked by the election, even when their prospects are under discussion.

Elections have such an impact on business, so it's no wonder that small business owners are interested in what politicians have to say.

That said, BDO's Business Trends report, finds that business optimism and output are still high, and that businesses are concerned about the long-term economic prospects of the UK.

A survey at the beginning of April 2015, just 5 weeks before the General Election, of FTSE 100 bosses showed that 70 per cent believe a Miliband government would be a 'catastrophe' for the economy

Read more: http://www.thisismoney.co.uk/money/markets/article-3029102/Who-spend-Labour-Conservative-economic-plans-hold-key-Number-Ten.html#ixzz3X5ZlAKZQ

However, no one is really sure where loyalties lie before or after an election, but keeping a keen eye on upcoming policies and campaigns are crucial in helping your business plan for any eventuality.

Fifteen - CYBERCRIME AND SMALL BUSINESS

A survey conducted by the UK government's Cyber Streetwise campaign has found that 66% of small and medium enterprises (SMEs) don't consider that their businesses might be vulnerable to a cyber attack.

Therefore only 16% say that they will commit to improving cyber security in 2015 and beyond.

This is a worrying trend, because even though many believe that only companies who take payments online are vulnerable to attack, this isn't the case. This is because small businesses often hold much more data than the average consumer, but without the same protections as big business, making SMEs a bigger target than ever before.

In this section, we'll give you the run down of the risks and provide tips for prevention and let you know what you should do if you're a victim of a cyberattack.

What could happen?

Last year alone (2014), 33% of small businesses fell victim to cyber attacks, most often initiated by someone outside of their business. With data from the Information Security Breaches Survey finding that the average cost of the worst security breach is between £65,000 - £115,000, on top of a business being out of action for around ten days, can you really afford not to pay attention to cyber security?

It seems that many businesses think that they can, as 24% of small businesses feel that it would be too expensive to implement cybersecurity measures, with 22% not knowing where to start. This lack of understanding surrounding cyber threats is extremely damaging to businesses, many of which are left vulnerable to losing data as well as suffering other knock-on effects.

John Allan, national chairman of the Federation of Small Businesses commented: *"We know from our own research that in the future small businesses expect to become much more dependent on web based tools. We also know that, as firms' reliance on tools like cloud computing increases, they also become more aware of the threats these services can pose".*

He went on to say, *"For example, nearly a third of businesses we questioned (61 per cent) were worried about the threat of data theft or loss. We need to give these businesses the knowledge and tools they require to prevent this from happening, and so help the continued take-up of these productivity-enhancing technologies."*

What can I do to protect myself?

There are a few steps you can take to begin to protect your business.

- ✓ **Encrypt your data:** Bank details, credit card information, national insurance numbers - are all pieces of data which hackers are after. Whenever important data is at rest, i.e. when you're not transmitting it over the internet, it should be encrypted.

- ✓ **Lock your network:** Known as 'war-driving', most victims of hacking are compromised through their Wi-Fi networks, which are often unsecured or vulnerable. The best defence is to use the less versatile but more secure wired networks, but if you really must use Wi-Fi, update it to the latest encryption standard and disable the SSID.

- ✓ **Use anti-virus software:** According to American telecommunications company Verizon, nearly half of the all data breaches use malware, which was responsible for almost 80% of the records stolen. Because this software often comes in via an email, the best way to prevent an attack in this form is to run anti-malware and anti-virus software after every software install.

- ✓ **Educate your employees:** You can't be the only one in your business who is vigilant about your cyber security, as it only takes one weak link. Keeping employees up to date about threats, as well as writing out a formal internet policy, will help employees know what is expected of them.

I've been hacked! What do I do?

In every situation, the very first thing to do is to **change passwords**, especially those with any administration rights. The next steps can alter depending on the type of attack you have suffered.

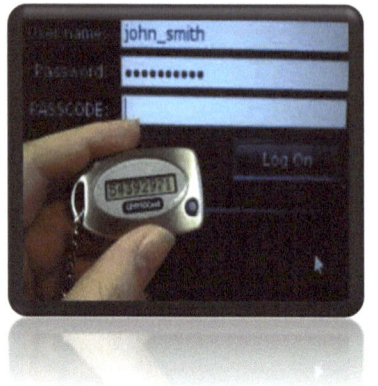

A common type of attack is to **redirect your website to something unsavoury.** If this happens, you'll need to get in contact with your web host to get things pointing the right way again.

However, if you have been the victim of 'ransomware', **where a computer is locked until a ransom is paid**, the computer should be disconnected from the network and shut down. If it won't let you do this, just pull the plug.

Regardless of the type of attack, you should always **report it to the police.** It may seem a pointless exercise, but law enforcement is getting increasingly better at dealing with hacking incidents. This may not help you directly in the short term, but the more hackers that are reported, the more they can be put out of business and the safer the online world can become, which is vital to small businesses.

However, as with most things, the **best defence is prevention.** If you are yet to review your cyber security procedure, or put into place a plan which details what you would do in the event of an attack, you're not only leaving yourself vulnerable to hackers but to the law too.

This is because if a hack takes place and is reported to the Information Commissioner's Office (ICO), your business could be fined if you are found to have handled data irresponsibly. So be warned!

Sixteen - BECOME AN HR HERO WITH HASSLE-FREE HIRING

There are plenty of options presented to you when you decide to take on staff in your small business. Often, small business owners and entrepreneurs will opt to hire a freelancer to complete a task. This can be a really positive step and lead to you saving not only money, but also time.

On the other hand, there are some positions that cry out to be filled by a full time member of staff. An employee can feel like they are better able to do their job if they are offered job security, long-term prospects and the opportunity to build relationships, and for you, you can foster loyalty and experience to benefit your business.

This tends to mean that permanent staff buy into company goals and values, and overall tend to have invested more in the success of the business. If you're considering taking on staff, it's generally a sign that your business is doing well. However, the process of hiring may seem like a bit of a minefield, so we've rounded up some of the most common questions and given you the answers to make you a hiring hero!

How can I save time?

There never seems to be enough time in the day, and this is especially true for those who run a small business. Therefore, taking valuable time out of your day to run a recruitment drive may seem counterproductive. However, from drafting up your job adverts, to making job offers, this isn't a process that should be rushed - taking your time will be worth it in the long run!

The best way to cut down your recruitment time is to slowly cultivate a 'talent pool' over time. Mike Ferguson, client relationship director at Social Media Search, says *"This can be done using social media such as LinkedIn or Twitter. This allows you to form the basis of a relationship with suitably qualified and experienced people and when you need to bring new talent into your business, you may already be in touch with them."*

You may also consider conducting phone or Skype interviews before inviting candidates to a formal interview, this way you can eliminate time-wasters or unsuitable candidates early on.

How can I be competitive?

It's true that small businesses may struggle to offer the same salaries as large firms, but they have an edge as they can offer other benefits.

As mentioned above, a large multi-national company may not be able to offer candidates flexible working hours, ability to work from home, or additional holiday, whereas a small business could.

Even offering performance-related bonuses are easier in a smaller firm, as you are fully aware of exactly how your employees are doing. But this doesn't mean you should assume that you know what is important to them, so try conducting a simple survey which can help you find out what motivates them. This way, you can build on establishing a strong workforce for the future.

How can I integrate my new-hire?

A personality clash that may be solved in a large firm by moving offices just isn't workable in small businesses and startups. Working together in small environments can cause issues and this means that making sure your new employee meshes well with your team is essential.

Most times, a proper induction will iron out any creases. This should include introductions to the team, making everyone's duties clear, and possibly even setting up a 'buddy' system for the first month or so.

Highlighting the reasons a new employee has joined the team should also help prevent others feel that their position is under threat. This is a common mistake made by many business owners and often leads to serious upsets amongst staff on day one, which then becomes a serious issue later on.

That's not to say you should hire identikit employees. Throwing a new personality and skill set into the mix could be what your company needs, and your team will always be more successful with a mix of characters who can balance each other out.

How do I let them know how they're getting on?

Sure, you still want to give feedback at the end of a probationary period, in fact this is often where the employee will know that their continuous employment is confirmed.

However, there is nothing wrong with having a review halfway through that period too, to give the employee an idea of what they are doing well, and what they could improve. You never know, they may pick up on the shortfalls you mention and turn them into strengths!

It's is always important to ensure, that both you and the new employee are absolutely clear on what their job role is and creating a clear job description is important. It's very easy in any walk of life, for two people to have different views on what was discussed and it's easy for either party to interpret a conversation differently.

By having a clear job description, both parties will fully understand what is expected of the new employee.

Without it, a new employee could easily turn around and say:

"I didn't realise that was what was expected of me", or
"I didn't know that was part of my job description".

Whether it's your first employee, or you've now got a small staff, hiring is always a big step for small business. Hopefully by answering a few common questions, I have helped you feel more prepared and in the driving seat when looking to hire.

Hire for your company's style

There's a reason why staff in a small business often feel like a family. The reason for this is because a team spends a lot of time working closely with each other, especially at the outset. The likelihood is that you will spend more time with your work colleagues than with your loved ones.

It's not only important that you like your employees but that your company likes your employees. Never forget this very important point.

In order for someone to fit your company culture, you don't only look at whether they'll get the office joke, you should also look at hiring people who are more highly skilled in their area than you are. This way you can have specific roles within your organisation for these people, and they will feel valued, fit in and part of the team.

Employees need to feel valued. If they don't you will never get the best out of them. Everyone needs to enjoy going to work and enjoy working for 'their' company.

Seventeen - WHERE CAN I GET HELP?

DAA Consulting offers business advice, consultancy as well as a free mentoring service for both start-ups and established businesses.

Based in Hertfordshire, all of DAA Consulting members have started, owned and run their own small business and a lot of the information in this book has been gleamed from their past experiences. They offer a wealth of knowledge and experience, as well as access to a large network of support.

Their members have 'been there, seen it and done it', so any advice given, will be from someone who understands what it really takes to run and manage a small business.

DAA Consultants are all accredited business advisors, many with the ibd-group, the Institute of Enterprise and Entrepreneurs, the Association of Business Mentors or Enterprise Nation as well as referral partners for Start-up Loans.

They can be contacted on **01707 527725** or by email at office@daa.consulting.

Thank you for reading and good luck with your venture.

"Whenever you see a successful business, someone once made a courageous decision."
— Peter F. Drucker

DAA Consulting

A David Anthony Ashdown book

www.daa.consulting

https://www.facebook.com/pages/DAA-Consulting/326130304259115

www.twitter.com/daaconsulting

uk.linkedin.com/pub/dir/DavidAshdown

DAA Consulting 11 Greenleaf House, Darkes Lane, Potters Bar, Herts. EN6 1AE

Tel: +44 (0)1707 527725 Fax: +44 (0)1707 658323

Email: office@daa.consulting Website: www.daa.consulting. First published in Great Britain in 2015. Copyright © David Anthony Ashdown, DAA Consulting.

The right of David Ashdown to be identified as Author has been asserted in accordance with the Copyright, Design and Patents Act 1988.

www.ingramcontent.com/pod-product-compliance
Lightning Source LLC
Chambersburg PA
CBHW040839180526

45159CB00001B/238